SENIOR SOURCE...

A Guide to Managing the Maze of Medicare

By John T. Sheerin

This book is dedicated to my wife and business partner Shannon, and my 3 children who have stuck with me through all the success, and all the failures.

Thank you for purchasing this book

Sign up for our mailing list to receive special updates, offers, and more information on how to protect your money.

www.SeniorSourceCT.com

Copyright

First published in the United States of America in 2019 by John T. Sheerin.

Edited by Mike and Maria Keiser

Artwork by Chris Todd

Pictures by John Garaventa

Copyright © The Senior Source, LLC 2019.

ISBN: 9781696749077

All rights are reserved. No part of this publication shall be reproduced, transmitted, or sold in whole or in part in any form without prior written consent of the author. All trademarks and registered trademarks appearing in this guide are the property of their respective owners.

Legalese

The information contained in this guide is for informational purposes only.

The material may include information, products, or services by third parties. As such, we do not assume responsibility or liability for any third-party material or opinions.

Readers are advised to do their own due diligence when it comes to making financial decisions. All mentioned information, products, and services should be independently verified by your own qualified professionals. By reading this guide, you agree that neither our company or I are responsible for the success or failure of your decisions relating to any information presented.

You may find different pathways to your success. I hope you'll consider sharing your success story with me at:

SeniorSource1@aol.com

First edition, October 2019.

Happy reading!

TABLE OF CONTENTS

Introduction: 7

Chapter 1: How Medicare Works ...9

Chapter 2: The Advantages and Disadvantages of each Medicare Plan Option..16

Chapter 3: Medicare Savings Programs 30

Chapter 4: Additional Coverage Options 35

Chapter 5: When You Are Eligible to Enroll in Medicare Plans 38

Conclusion: 44

Acknowledgements......................45

About the Author 46

Want More?..................................48

INTRODUCTION

Navigating Medicare can be a daunting task. Whether you're just turning 65 or currently on Medicare and considering all your options, my goal for this book is to help you get a clear understanding of Medicare, how it works, your options, and how to make the right choice. It is important to understand your Medicare coverage choices and to pick your coverage carefully. How you choose to get your benefits and who you get them from can affect your out-of-pocket costs and where you can get your care.

In this book, I'm going to explain to you how Medicare works, all the different components of Medicare, the coverage choices you have, the advantages and disadvantages to each, hospital indemnity, and additional options that may be available to you.

My goal for you reading this book is that you'll have a clear understanding of Medicare and the options that best fit your life.

This book is meant to be a guide. I wanted to simplify and clarify Medicare for you. However, before you make any decisions, please consult with a professional financial advisor that specializes in Medicare policies.

CHAPTER 1

How Medicare Works

A person becomes eligible to receive health benefits under Medicare in 2 ways:

- By turning 65
- Through Social Security Disability

Learning the Medicare lingo is the first step in understanding how Medicare works. There are lots of letters, plan names and new terms to understand. We want you to feel like you have a good grasp on Medicare so you can choose a plan that's right for you. This chapter will help you understand the common terms and how the different types of Medicare plans on the market compare to each other.

Defining Parts A, B, C and D

Medicare has four parts. Parts A and B are called original Medicare or traditional Medicare. They're run by the federal government. Medicare Part C is called Medicare Advantage. You buy Medicare Advantage plans from private health insurance companies that contract with the government. They work with Medicare and your coverage would come from a private insurance company rather than traditional Medicare. Part D covers prescription drugs. Many Medicare Advantage plans combine Parts A, B and D in one plan. And each Medicare plan only covers one person, not a married couple.

There is no cost to the individual for Medicare Part A. However, there will generally be monthly premium for Part B. It's usually taken out of your monthly social security payment. However, if you're not currently receiving social security, you will be billed quarterly for your premium.

Here's an overview of some of the things each part covers:

Medicare Part A is hospital coverage that helps cover the costs for:

- Inpatient care in a hospital or skilled nursing facility (not long-term care)
- Hospice and some home health care services post hospital or skilled nursing facility stay
- There is no premium that the individual must pay for Medicare Part A

Medicare Part B is medical coverage that helps cover the cost of:

- Doctor services, hospital outpatient care, and some home health care services, as well as lab tests and durable medical equipment
- Most preventative services, including an annual wellness exam
- The individual does pay a monthly premium for Medicare Part B, usually around $135 per month (2019 rate). It is typically taken from your social security check. If you are not yet on Medicare, you will be billed quarterly for your Part B.
- There are some circumstances where you may qualify to receive Part B at no cost. We'll cover this in a later chapter. However, approximately 85% of recipients pay for Part B.
- There is a small percentage who may have to pay more than $135 (2019 rate).
    - As of 2019 the limits are
        - Folks with individual income over $85K
        - Couples with income over $170K

Medicare Part C, also called Medicare Advantage

- Includes all benefits and services covered under parts A and B (and usually Part D)
- Provided by private health insurance companies
- Requires annual enrollment
- May have a provider or facility network

When Advantage plans came into being, insurance companies worked directly with Medicare to develop Part C, Medicare Advantage plans. To join an Advantage plan, you must already have Parts A and B. You no longer would use your Medicare card for healthcare. Your sole provider is the private insurance company. The government contracts with the private insurance carriers and pays a fixed fee per person to the insurance companies. Medicare likes the idea of the fixed cost and insurance companies believe they can control costs better than the government can.

Medicare Part D is a stand-alone prescription drug coverage that:

- Helps pay for many brand-name and generic prescribed drugs

- Often gives you access to mail order options and retail drug stores across the country

Traditional Medicare (Parts A & B) with a Supplement, also known as Medigap

Medigap, otherwise known as a Medicare supplement, is extra health insurance that you buy from a private company to pay health care costs not covered by traditional Medicare, such as co-payments, deductibles, and health care if you travel outside the U.S. Medigap policies don't cover long-term care, dental care, vision care, hearing aids, eyeglasses, and private-duty nursing. Most plans do not cover prescription drugs, unless they fall under Part B. Ask your Insurance Professional about this.

You pay a monthly premium for a Medigap policy. A Medigap policy covers only one person. If you and your spouse both want a Medigap policy, you will each need to buy one. Some Insurance companies offer discounts when couples apply.

Medigap policies are only available to people who already have Medicare Parts A and B. People who have a Medicare Advantage plan cannot get a Medigap plan.

Medigap plans were standardized in 1992. There are plans A-N. Medigap plan A would have limited coverage while a plan such as N would offer more comprehensive coverage. With each plan, there will still be some deductible and co-pays. Since these plans were standardized, each plan has identical coverage across insurance carriers.

In chapter 5, I'll discuss the different times you are eligible to enroll in Medicare and Medicare Advantage plans.

In the next chapter, we'll cover the advantages and disadvantages of each plan.

Medicare Plans

Plan A	For Hospital Coverage
Plan B	For Medical Coverage
Plan C	Also called Medicare Advantage
Plan D	Prescription Drug Coverage

Notes:

Chapter 2

The Advantages and Disadvantages of each Medicare Plan Option

The advantages of traditional Medicare

The first advantage of traditional Medicare is that there is no charge to the individual for Medicare Part A. As I mentioned, there is a monthly premium for Part B.

There are no lifetime limits on healthcare with traditional Medicare

Traditional Medicare is completely transferrable. You can go to any doctor in any network that accepts Medicare. There are no referrals needed either. Again, if the doctor accepts Medicare, you may go to them.

If you travel a lot or spend your winters somewhere else, traditional Medicare might be the best option for you.

Traditional Medicare will cover 80% of the costs of healthcare for Parts A and B. However, as we mentioned, Part D coverage is a separate policy.

When you combine Tradition Medicare with a Medigap policy, most of your healthcare is typically covered (not prescriptions), although there may be some co-pays and deductibles.

The disadvantages of traditional Medicare

There are a few disadvantages of a traditional Medicare plan.

Traditional Medicare plans don't include a prescription drug plan. You need to purchase a separate Part D plan. The premium for Part D can cost anywhere between $30 - $220 per month.

Other costs can be prohibitive. Even with a Medigap (supplement) policy, there can still be considerable co-pays and deductibles, depending on the level of Medigap policy that you purchase.

Also, as I mentioned before, there are no vision, dental, or hearing benefits with a traditional plan, even when you purchase a supplement.

However, there are situations where having a traditional plan with a supplement and a Part D policy makes sense. Again, people who travel a lot or live out of state part of the year would be a good example. I also find that it is generally people 80 years old and over who opt for this plan.

Compare Medigap policies

If a percentage appears, the Medigap plan covers that percentage of the benefit, and you are responsible for the rest.

Medicare Supplement Insurance (Medigap Plans)

Benefits	A	B	C	D	F*	G	K	L	M	N
Medicare Part A coinsurance and hospital costs (up to an additional 365 days after Medicare benefits are used)	100%	100%	100%	100%	100%	100%	100%	100%	100%	100%
Medicare Part B coinsurance or copayment	100%	100%	100%	100%	100%	100%	50%	75%	100%	100%****
Blood (first 3 pints)	100%	100%	100%	100%	100%	100%	50%	75%	100%	100%
Part A hospice care coinsurance or copayment	100%	100%	100%	100%	100%	100%	50%	75%	100%	100%
Skilled nursing facility care coinsurance			100%	100%	100%	100%	50%	75%	100%	100%
Part A deductible		100%	100%	100%	100%	100%	50%	75%	50%	100%
Part B deductible			100%		100%					
Part B excess charges					100%	100%				
Foreign travel emergency (up to plan limits)			80%	80%	80%	80%			80%	80%

*Plan F also offers a high-deductible plan in some states. With this option, you must pay for Medicare-covered costs (Coinsurance, copayments, and deductibles) up to the deductible amount of $2300 in 2019 before your policy pays anything. (Plans C and F won't be available to people who are newly eligible for Medicare on or after January 1, 2020.

**For Plans K and L, after you meet your out-of-pocket yearly limit and your yearly Part B deductible, the Medigap plan pays 100% of covered services for the rest of the calendar year.

***Plan N pays 1% of the Part B coinsurance, except for a copayment of up to $ for some office visits and up to $50 copayment for emergency room visits that don't result in an inpatient admission.

Advantages of a Medicare Part C (Medicare Advantage) Plan

Medicare Advantage, also known as Medicare Part C, makes it possible for people with Medicare Part A (hospital insurance) and Part B (medical insurance) to receive their Medicare benefits in an alternative way. Medicare Advantage plans are offered by private insurance companies contracted with Medicare and provide at least the same level of coverage that Medicare Part A and Part B provide.

You may be wondering which is the better choice: sign up for a Medicare Advantage plan or Original Medicare. There isn't a simple answer because Medicare Advantage plans have key features that many people find attractive and other characteristics that may not match with your personal preferences and/or lifestyle. Let's take a closer look at some of the important pros and cons of Medicare Advantage plans.

Medicare Advantage plans often provide more benefits than you would receive under Original Medicare.

Medicare Advantage plans must offer at least the same level of coverage as Medicare Part A and Part B and many plans offer added benefits. These may include coverage for routine vision care, hearing aids, routine dental care, prescription drug coverage, and fitness center membership.

Medicare Advantage plans may cost you less.

If you enroll in a Medicare Advantage plan, some plans may have premiums as low as $0.

Your cost sharing may also be less under Medicare Advantage. For, example, if you visit a primary care physician under Medicare Advantage, you may pay a copayment of $10. However, if you visit a primary care physician under Original Medicare, you may have a coinsurance of 20%, which could be more than $10.

Also, a Medicare Advantage plan limits your maximum out-of-pocket expense. Once you have spent that maximum, you pay nothing for covered medical services for the remainder of the year. Original Medicare does not provide a maximum out-of-pocket cap, so your potential expenses are limitless.

Often a Medicare Advantage plan can be less expensive than comparable coverage you would receive if you stayed with Original Medicare. To get all the benefits of Medicare Advantage with Original Medicare, you would also need to enroll in a stand-alone Medicare

Part D Prescription Drug Plan as well as a Medicare Supplement plan.

Medicare Advantage plans coordinate care among your health care providers.

Typically, Medicare Advantage plans are managed care and have networks of contracted health care providers. Example would be Health Maintenance Organization (HMO) Medicare Advantage plans. These HMO plans require you to select a Primary Care Physician (PCP) who helps to coordinate your care.

Medicare Advantage plans that include prescription drug coverage may also have medication therapy management. This care coordination can be a convenience and a valuable aid to your health.

Medicare Advantage plans that will allow you to go outside of your network.

Preferred Provider Organization (PPO) Plan

PPO plans have network doctors, other health care providers, and hospitals, but will also cover out-of-network providers for a higher cost.

** Please note: You are always covered for emergency and urgent care

There are also other advantages to this type of plan

- Some PPO plans offer prescription drug coverage.
- You don't need to choose a primary care doctor
- In most cases you don't have to get a referral to see a specialist

Private Fee-for-Service (PFFS) Plan

A PFFS plan allows you to go to any Medicare-approved doctor, other health care provider, or hospital that accepts the plan's payment terms and agrees to treat you. If you join a PFFS plan that has a network, you can also see any o the network providers who have agreed to always treat plan members. Additionally, you can choose an out-of-network doctor, hospital, or other provider who accepts the plan's terms, you just may have to pay more. PFFS plans don't offer drug coverage, but you can join a Medicare Prescription Drug Plan to get the coverage you need.

Additional Benefits:

- You don't need to choose a primary care doctor
- You don't have to get a referral to see a specialist

Other things you should know about this plan

- The plan decides how much you pay for services and will tell you about your cost sharing in the "Annual Notice of Change" (ANOC) and "Evidence of Coverage" (EOC) documents that it sends out each year.
- Some PFFS plans contract with a network of providers who agree to always treat you, even if you have never seen them before.
- Out-of-network doctors, hospitals, and other providers may decide not to treat you, even if you have seen them before.
- Always show your plan member card before any treatment or service.
- In medical emergencies, doctors, hospitals, and other providers must treat you.

Medicare Advantage plans can serve as your "one-stop" center for all your health and prescription drug coverage needs.

Most Medicare Advantage plans combine medical and Part D prescription drug coverage. Many also coordinate the delivery of added benefits, such as vision, dental, and hearing care. You may prefer the convenience of working with one plan administrator.

Disadvantages of a Medicare Part C (Medicare Advantage) Plan

Medicare Advantage plans may limit your freedom of choice in health care providers

With the federally administered Medicare program, you can generally go to any doctor or facility that accepts Medicare and receive the same level of Medicare benefits for covered services. In contrast, Medicare Advantage plans are more restricted in terms of their provider networks. If you go out of network, your plan may not cover your medical costs, or your costs may not apply to your out of pocket maximum. And some Medicare Advantage plans will still have deductibles and co-pays for certain procedures and visits.

Medicare Advantage plans' coverage for some services and procedures may require doctor's referral and plan authorizations.

Medicare Advantage plans try to prevent the misuse or overuse of health care through various means. This might include prior authorization for hospital stays, home health care, medical equipment, and certain complicated procedures. Medicare Advantage plans may also require your primary care doctor's referral to see specialists before they will pay for services.

Medicare Advantage plans have specific service areas.

Most Medicare Advantage plans have regional (rather than nationwide) networks of participating providers. To enroll, you must reside in the Medicare Advantage plan's service area at least 6 months of the year. If you divide your time between homes located in different areas, this requirement may be difficult to meet.

The bottom line is that Medicare Advantage plans may provide more affordable coverage than you would receive otherwise. The trade-off is that you must follow the Medicare

Advantage plan's rules to receive payment for covered services.

Notes:

Chapter 3

Medicare Savings Programs

Medicare Savings Programs (MSP) are federally funded programs administered by each individual state. These programs are for people with limited income and resources and help pay some or all of their Medicare premiums, deductibles, copayments and coinsurance.

There are three Medicare Savings Programs:

- Qualified Medicare Beneficiary (QMB);
- Specified Low-Income Medicare Beneficiary (SLMB)
- Additional Low-Income Medicare Beneficiary (ALMB)

Requirements to qualify for a Medicare Savings Program

Here are a few of the general requirements for the MSP:

- Age 65 or older
- Receive Social Security Disability benefits
- People with certain disabilities or permanent kidney failure (even if under age 65)

- Or you meet standard income and resource requirements

For a full list of requirements visit Medicare.gov Medicare Savings Program page. Direct Link: https://www.medicare.gov/your-medicare-costs/get-help-paying-costs

Only the state can determine if an individual qualifies for coverage under one of the programs. Many states apply different standards and methods to determine MSP eligibility. Some states, for example, have no resources for these programs or figure the income and resources differently.

I'll talk specifically about Connecticut's Medicare savings program.

Connecticut's Medicare Savings programs are administered by the Connecticut Department of Social Services (DSS). To apply, complete a short application form. Call CHOICES at 1-800-994-9422, visit your local DSS office, or go to http://portal.ct.gov/dss for an application.

QMB, SLMB, and ALMB benefits usually start the month after you apply. In certain cases, SLMB and ALMB benefits are granted up to 3 months *before* you apply. This means you could get back up to 3 months' worth of all or some of the premiums that you paid out before you applied.

If I'm eligible for the QMB program, do I need Medigap insurance?

If you get Medicare and you are enrolled in an Original Medicare Program (fee for service), you can purchase a Medicare Supplemental Insurance (Medigap) policy to help pay some of the health care costs that Medicare does not cover.

The QMB program offers most of the benefits of Medigap policies **if you visit medical providers who accept both Medicare and Medicaid**. Before you cancel your Medigap insurance, make sure your medical providers accept both Medicare and Medicaid. If your QMB coverage ends, you may be able to reinstate your former Medigap policy.

Important Note: SLMB and ALMB programs do not offer the benefits of Medigap insurance. If you are enrolled in the Original Medicare Program, you should not cancel your Medigap policy when you enroll in the SLMB or ALMB programs.

As I mentioned at the beginning of the book, please speak with a professional financial advisor who specializes in Medicare before making any decisions.

Notes:

Chapter 4

Additional Coverage Options

A lot of my clients are concerned about out of pocket costs and things that are not covered under their plans, whether they are in traditional Medicare or a Medicare Advantage plan.

Sometimes, even with Medicare, certain things are not covered, such as, dental, vision, or hearing. There are private insurance policies that are available to you if any of these things are not covered by your Medicare plan. And many of these plans are not terribly expensive.

One of the bigger concerns my clients who have a Medicare Advantage plan have are the hospital co-pays. The average co-pay is $450 per day for the first 4 days. This can be a daunting amount of money for some people. There are plans available called a Hospital Indemnity Plan that will cover all the co-pays if you end up in the hospital.

Hospital Indemnity insurance, also called Hospitalization insurance or Hospital insurance, is a plan that pays you benefits when you are confined to a hospital, whether for planned or unplanned reasons, or for other medical services, depending on the policy.

Hospital stays can strain even the healthiest of budgets. And in many cases, you can't ignore the care you need even if it pushes you financially. Hospital Indemnity insurance plans provide payment for each day spent in the hospital, and for some other qualified expenses as well. That's money you can use as you choose, whether for hospital bills or those other costs that come up while you're recovering.

A typical hospital indemnity plan is approximately $45 per month.

Notes:

CHAPTER 5

When You Are Eligible to Enroll in Medicare Plans

There are only certain times during the year when you are eligible to enroll or make changes to your Medicare plan.

First, there's the **Initial Enrollment Period.**

This refers to you aging into Medicare, ie, turning 65. You have 3 months before your 65th birthday until 3 months after your 65th birthday to initially enroll in Medicare.

Annual Enrollment Period

The Annual Enrollment Period, otherwise referred to as AEP, is the time of year when a Medicare beneficiary can make plan changes. The fall AEP runs from October 15th to December 7th.

During AEP, the plan benefit changes for the next year are released, allowing Medicare beneficiaries to look around to ensure they are electing the plan that best fits their needs.

What You Can do During the Fall Annual Enrollment Period

During the Annual Enrollment Period, Medicare Beneficiaries can elect to any of the following:

- Drop a Medicare Advantage Plan and return to Original Medicare
- Elect to change from one Medicare Advantage plan to a different one
- Change from Original Medicare to a Medicare Advantage plan
- Elect to change from one Part D prescription drug plan to another
- Cancel your current Part D plan
- Pick up a Part D Plan if you currently do not have one

Any changes you make during the AEP will go into effect on January 1st of the following year.

With Medicare Advantage and Part D plan benefits changing every year, premiums could increase, benefits can be changed, and prescription drug formularies can be changed. A formulary is a list of approved medications the plan will cover.

The AEP gives you a chance to change if you are not happy with the future adjustments to your plan.

Open Enrollment Period

The Open Enrollment Period (OEP) runs from January 1 until March 31.

What You Can Do During OEP

OEP vs AEP Medicare is very different. In the Open Enrollment Period beneficiaries currently enrolled in a Medicare Advantage Plan can:

- Cancel your stand-alone Part D prescription drug plan
- Drop your Medicare Advantage Plan and return to Original Medicare
- Enroll in a stand-alone Medicare Part D prescription drug plan
- Elect to change from one Medicare Advantage Plan to another

Regarding enrolling in a stand-alone Part D plan... most Medicare Advantage Plans include prescription coverage. Once you sign up with a Part D plan, the dis-enrollment from Medicare Advantage Plan happens automatically and return you to Medicare Part A and Part B.

You can enroll in a Medicare Supplement Plan (Medigap) once you are disenrolled from your Medicare Advantage Plan if you can medically qualify.

One Chance to Make Changes

You only get one chance to make an election during the OEP. Once the election has been made you cannot change it again until the next AEP.

If you decide to make a change, it will go into effect the following month. For example, a plan change on January 5th would start on February 1st.

There are many reasons that a beneficiary may want to change from the plan they are enrolled in using this election period.

Below are some of the reasons someone may choose to change:

- Provider network changes
- Dental coverage provided isn't as comprehensive
- Certain benefits covered at 80% such as chemotherapy, durable medical equipment, and Part B drugs

Special Enrollment Period

There are some special circumstances when you can make changes to your Medicare plan outside of the normal enrollment periods. This is known as a special enrollment period. A few of these circumstances would be:

- You're moving from 1 state to another
- You are still working, and an insurance policy is changing
- You become eligible for the Medicare Savings Program

There are many others, but I wanted to share a few examples with you. During the special enrollment periods, you have 60 days to make the changes to your plan.

Notes

Conclusion

I hope that I've accomplished my goal of providing you with a basic understand of how Medicare works. I realize it can be confusing. So please use this book as a reference guide that you can refer to whenever you want.

With Medicare Advantage, there are a lot of different companies offering a lot of different plans. It can be a challenge to figure out which is the best plan for you.

Then there's also the decision to go with Medicare Advantage or stick with traditional Medicare.

** Important: 90 days prior to having to make any decisions, I would strongly urge you to reach out to a financial advisor that specializes in Medicare to discuss all your options with you.

Thank you for reading this book and I wish you the best.

Acknowledgements

There are many people that helped make this book a reality. I want to take this opportunity to thank my "Village".

A special thank you to my wife and business partner Shannon who has supported my efforts throughout my career.

To Bobbi for all her hard work.

To Marc who brought me into the business.

To my mom who has always been there when I needed her.

And of course, my children. The reason I strive to improve every day.

About the Author

John T. Sheerin, a native of

Stamford, CT, graduated from Central Connecticut State University in 1992 with a degree in Business Management. He began his career with a major insurance company in September of that year. He then advanced into the area of training, and achieved manager status in 1996, overseeing a sales force of 35 agents.

During his tenure, he developed an extensive clientele of seniors, advising them in the areas of Medicare, Life Insurance, and Annuity investments. He is certified by Connecticut Partnership for Long-Term Care.

John has more than 27 years of experience in helping and advising seniors in the areas of:

- Medicare Planning
- Secure Investments
- Preservation of Assets and Income
- Medical and Life Insurance
- Estate Planning

About The Senior Source

While most financial service firms attempt to be everything to everyone, The Senior Source focuses exclusively on the needs of those in and nearing retirement age and with their specific financial needs and opportunities. We are a professional firm designed to assist seniors in protecting their assets and standard of living.

WANT MORE?

We hope you have enjoyed this book; it is our hope that the information provided for you helps you

If you enjoyed this book and want to learn more, please contact us.

The Senior Source
141 Hazard Avenue
Enfield, CT 06082
860-525-0414
SeniorSource1@aol.com
www.SeniorSourceCT

www.ingramcontent.com/pod-product-compliance
Lightning Source LLC
Chambersburg PA
CBHW070859220526
45466CB00005B/2045